LAWRENCE "J" WALKER III

Crypto Your Mind

Learn The Basics of Cryptocurrency

Copyright © 2020 by Lawrence "J" Walker III

All rights reserved. No part of this publication may be reproduced, stored or transmitted in any form or by any means, electronic, mechanical, photocopying, recording, scanning, or otherwise without written permission from the publisher. It is illegal to copy this book, post it to a website, or distribute it by any other means without permission.

Lawrence "J" Walker III asserts the moral right to be identified as the author of this work.

Lawrence "J" Walker III has no responsibility for the persistence or accuracy of URLs for external or third-party Internet Websites referred to in this publication and does not guarantee that any content on such Websites is, or will remain, accurate or appropriate.

Designations used by companies to distinguish their products are often claimed as trademarks. All brand names and product names used in this book and on its cover are trade names, service marks, trademarks and registered trademarks of their respective owners. The publishers and the book are not associated with any product or vendor mentioned in this book. None of the companies referenced within the book have endorsed the book.

This book is meant to inform and not suggesting what cryptocurrencies to buy. Invest in cryptocurrencies at your own risk.

First edition

Illustration by Taneya Walker

*This book was professionally typeset on Reedsy.
Find out more at reedsy.com*

Contents

Preface	iv
Acknowledgement	viii
1 Chapter 1: THE BASICS	1
What Is Cryptocurrency?	1
What Is Decentralization?	2
What Is Blockchain?	3
What Is Bitcoin?	5
Who Is Satoshi Nakamoto?	8
What Is a Satoshi?	9
What Are Altcoins?	10
Tokens vs Coins	11
What Are Stablecoins?	13
2 Chapter 2: SMART CONTRACTS AND MINING	17
What Is a Smart Contract?	17
What Is Mining?	20
What Is Proof of Work (PoW)?	22
What Is Proof of Stake (PoS)?	22
3 Chapter 3: CRYPTO AND FIAT MENTALITIES	26
Different Mentalities	26
How Money is Trusted as an Exchange of Value	28
4 Chapter 4: BUYING AND SELLING	32
Buying and Selling	32
Trading Pairs	33
Common Buying Scenario	34
Exchanges	35

	Security on Exchanges	36
	Where to Buy Your Crypto	36
	Withdrawal Fees	37
	Decentralized Exchanges	38
5	Chapter 5: STORING YOUR CRYPTOCURRENCY	39
	Storing Your Cryptocurrency	39
	Surface Level: Wallets, Private Keys, Public Addresses	41
	A Little Deeper: Wallets	42
	Sending Crypto	44
	A Little Deeper: Private Keys and Public Addresses	44
	Backing Up Private Keys, Public Address, Password, and Recovery Passphrases	45
	Blockchain Explorer	46
6	Chapter 6: ADVICE	48
	Advice, But Not Financial Advice	48
	Do Your Own Research	50
7	Chapter 7: INVESTMENT STRATEGIES	55
	Trading and Holding	55
	Trading	55
	Holding	57
	Taxes	58
	How to Cash Out	60
	Cash Out Spreadsheet	61
	How I'm Investing in Bitcoin	63
8	Chapter 8: CRYPTOCURRENCY METRICS	65
	Cryptocurrency Metrics	65
	How To Use These Data Points	66
	Price	68
9	Chapter 9: FIAT VS CRYPTOCURRENCY	71
	Crypto During the Pandemic	71

"Printing Money"	72
Cryptocurrency Is Just Easier	73
10 Chapter 10: CRYPTO DEFINITIONS AND SLANG	78
Cryptocurrency Defintions	78
Cryptocurrency Slang	83
About the Author	89

Preface

The purpose of me writing this book is to inform as many people as possible about the basics of cryptocurrency. I intend to only touch on the basics, so that it is easier for you to understand. If you understand, then you will have the knowledge and be able to participate in the world of cryptocurrency. If you are knowledgeable and participate now, you are an early participant and have an advantage over most people in this world. Cryptocurrency is something that the whole world will participate in soon.

Cryptocurrency and blockchain technology are the future of money and technology in this world. It is growing fast and you should be informed so that you don't miss out. Many compare this time to the internet wave in the early 90's. This past decade and these coming decades are a rare time in human history, where there will be a transition from one kind of currency (paper money, coins, and credit cards) to a new type of currency (cryptocurrency). But never before has the new currency come with new technology (blockchain). Most people who have lived on this earth have never seen a transition like it. It is extremely rare.

Cryptocurrency can get really complicated if you get into the fine details of how the technology works, but in this book we won't go there. Most people who invest don't even know the details of how the technology works. If you know the basics, that is enough to be effective.

Also this is an incredible opportunity to gain generational wealth. And I want as many people as possible to get in early. Especially the poor to middle class. Cryptocurrency has only been around for 11 years and is still in its early stages. If you get educated in at least the basics, you will have an incredible advantage over billions of people in the world. Most people don't know or even care about what cryptocurrency is. But they will be using it in the coming years. Many believe it is just a scam or only used by criminals; as if criminals don't use cash or credit cards to commit crimes every day. You can then use this advantage to potentially invest smartly in certain cryptocurrencies and gain financial freedom.

I want to inform the uninformed majority of the world about the basics of cryptocurrency. I want to excite you about the new world of cryptocurrency and inspire you to be an early adopter if you choose. This book should not be seen as financial advice. I may express ideas or have suggestions, but I am not an investment professional. Do your own research before you invest in anything, including cryptocurrency.

In full disclosure, in this book I mention the name of some cryptocurrencies that I have personally invested in (Bitcoin, Cardano, and UTRUST). I simply mention them to better explain my points because I am familiar with them. Let's get started!

Ideology Behind The Purpose of Cryptocurrency

Bitcoin is only 11 years old and so is the cryptocurrency market. Those of us that love this idea of decentralization and a new form of money believe that Bitcoin and some other cryptos are here to stay. But as a crypto newby, you are reading this book because you are curious and at least want to know the basics. If Bitcoin and some other cryptos continue to thrive and become adopted by the public, you have the chance to become wealthy, or at least be more prepared for the direction this world is going into. For example, if you buy $10 worth of bitcoin at $5,000 a coin, it may not be much. But your $10 will definitely get you way more bitcoin now than it will 5 years from now when the bitcoin price could be 50k or more. The people buying in at that point will not get as much for their money as you will now. This gives you an advantage.

Be the person who invested in Apple when it was a young promising company. Be the person who bought some shares of Microsoft in the early 90's. Cryptocurrency has the chance to be way more valuable than these examples, because we are talking about a new form of money and a new technology called blockchain.

Why cryptocurrency? What is so special about it? My dollars and credit card work just fine. These are common questions, and you will understand more as you read. But cryptocurrency is needed because it is built with all people in mind. Although many people in the world have access to a traditional bank. Not all people do. The current financial system leaves out too many people. 1.7 billion adults aren't involved in the world financial system and don't have access to a traditional bank. But more than 5 billion people in the world have a mobile device, and between 3.5 and 4.5 billion people use the internet. So digital currency will give more people around the world access to the financial system. There is still room for us to make the world financial system better and to include more people. Digital currency is the perfect way to do it. Especially by using mobile phones and the internet.

Other reasons why cryptocurrency and blockchain technology are needed:

- Cryptocurrency allows peer to peer transactions without the need of a third party (bank, government).
- Less fees that eat into your money.
- An open ledger of transactions for anybody to see. All transactions have a hash number so your name isn't attached to a transaction.
- Borderless transactions so you can send money or data to anybody in the world in seconds anytime you want with extremely minimal fees.

These are just some of the reasons why cryptocurrency and blockchain technology will be needed now, and into the future.

Acknowledgement

I would like to thank God, his son Jesus, and the Holy Spirit for always being there for me. Thank yah! I would also like to thank my wife Taneya for understanding why I stay up so late to write this book and supporting me. My son Dominic for hyping me up and putting his fingers to his temple and yelling "Crypto Your Mind." My mom and dad Barbara and Jarvis for working hard to put me in the positive position I am in life. My brother Warren for introducing me to cryptocurrency. My sister Sandy for hyping me up about writing this book. My niece and nephew Paige and Xavier for being part of the motivation to create generational wealth. And all my extended family, especially Uncle Johnnie, and the Ft. Lauderdale crew. Thank you Suppoman, Crypto Daily, Altcoin Daily, and Crypto Crow from YouTube for motivating me and leading me in the direction to get educated on all things crypto.

1

Chapter 1: THE BASICS

What Is Cryptocurrency?

Cryptocurrency is a digital currency. It uses encryption techniques to control the creation of monetary units called coins or tokens. Most cryptocurrencies are decentralized, which means it is not regulated or controlled by any third party, like a bank or government. Decentralization is one of the aspects of cryptocurrency that gives it value and separates it from fiat (government controlled money like US dollars.) There is no single point of failure with decentralization. Decentralized cryptocurrencies have several computers called nodes all around the world that validate the transactions of cryptocurrencies. These nodes store the cryptos data on the blockchain. Since there is no single point of failure, decentralized cryptocurrencies can't be shut down and some are censorship resistant. Not all cryptocurrencies are decentralized. But most are. And even though cryptocurrency is a digital currency, not all cryptocurrencies are used or created to be a currency. I will get more into that later.

What Is Decentralization?

Decentralization is one of the key elements that make cryptocurrency valuable. Decentralization is the concept of taking power away from a central authority. It puts that power in the hands of the people. No bank, no government, and no other third party involvement. That means having your money in your possession and not in the bank. Being able to do things like send bitcoin to your friends without having to deal with the bank's hours, fees, daily or monthly withdrawal limits, or down server time. With decentralization you can send crypto while being anonymous, yet the transaction is on the blockchain for anybody to see. Transparency is key to the blockchain. No hacking, no tampering.

You have to remember that the blockchain was invented after the financial crisis in 2008. At that time the people did not have a lot of trust in financial institutions. With decentralization, you don't have to worry about corrupt people or institutions making greedy and bad decisions that will intentionally or unintentionally affect your money. So blockchain uses the concept of decentralization to take that power from these financial institutions and put it in our own hands by only having to trust the blockchain. You may be thinking, so I should take my trust from the humans and give it to the blockchain software? Yes, you should. Because the blockchain can't be corrupted like human beings can. It only executes what is agreed upon by its protocols, and we can trust it to execute transactions without a third party being involved. This is decentralization. The decentralization aspect of the blockchain connects the people directly to each other.

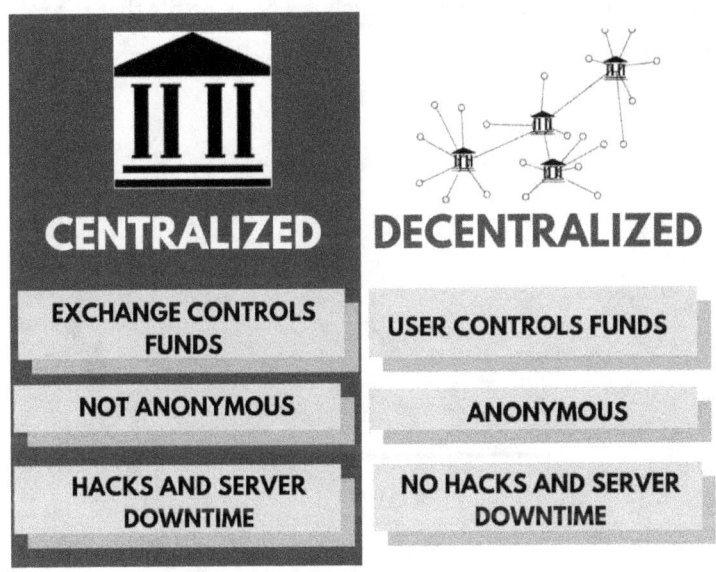

The main differences between centralized and decentralized systems.

What Is Blockchain?

Blockchain is a trusted network of computers called nodes that all have the same history of transactions. Instead of there being one company or one database that holds all the information, the same data is held by several nodes all over the world. When there is a new transaction, it is broadcast to a peer to peer network of nodes, and the nodes verify the transaction. Once verified, the transaction is added to the list of other transactions to create a new "block" of data on the blockchain. This new "block" is permanent and unalterable. Which means nobody can manipulate the data on the blockchain. The blockchain is often compared to a ledger; which is a book or file that records transactions.

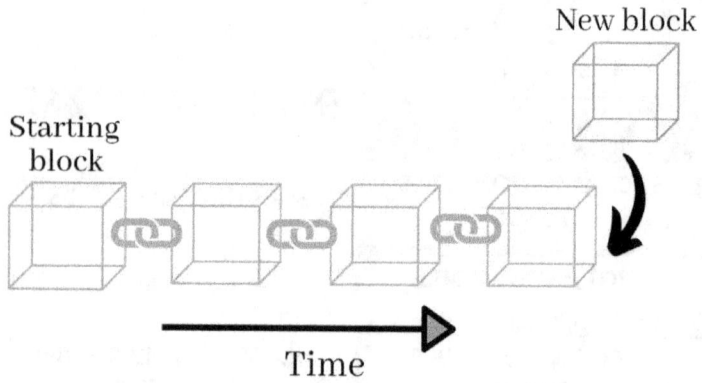

A new permanent and unalterable block is added to the blockchain after being verified.

Blockchain is a decentralized database. It is an underlying software that you will not see. It is the technology that powers cryptocurrencies, decentralized apps, websites, interfaces, etc. You will only see what comes from the blockchain, you will not see the blockchain itself.

What makes blockchain work is the idea of group consensus. Which means that thousands of these computer nodes must all have a copy of the same data. And the reason the nodes must have the same data is because if all or most of these thousands of computer nodes agree on having the same data, then what they agree on must be the truth. With consensus, the nodes go with whatever the majority agrees with. When they agree, the transaction is verified, and a new block of data is created that can't be changed. So, consensus is the core of what makes the blockchain work. This is what replaces the bank, middleman, or any other third party. Group consensus of the nodes on the blockchain prevents errors like double spending or fraud. Which is why consensus is important and very applicable to cryptocurrency.

Nodes come in many different forms. Nodes can be powerful computers, regular computers like your laptop, a small device that you can connect to your computer, an app on your phone, or a website.

See a video explanation of what blockchain is on Instagram and Twitter @CryptoYourMind.

What Is Bitcoin?

Bitcoin is the first cryptocurrency ever created. It is often referred to as digital gold. It is seen as a store of value. It was invented in 2009 by Satoshi Nakomoto after the financial crisis that caused the recession. Satoshi saw how so few powerful entities, having too much control over our money caused this problem. So, he or she created Bitcoin as a way for all people around the world to exchange money without relying on a third party to execute the transactions. The blockchain handles those transactions. The idea of Bitcoin is to put the power back into the hands of the people and out of the hands of banks and away from government restrictions.

Bitcoin is the most popular cryptocurrency. It's also the most valuable and the number 1 ranked cryptocurrency as far as market capitalization. Anybody who has heard of cryptocurrency has most likely also heard of Bitcoin. Out of all the 5,000 plus cryptocurrencies, Bitcoin has the most promise to last the test of time. It has done incredibly well so far. Even though it is very volatile because of its low supply, if you look at a chart of bitcoin over the past 11 years, it is on a steady rise. It continues to reach higher low price points and higher high price points. Which basically means the price may go up and down, but it has generally been going in a healthy upward rise since it was created. Bitcoin has more trust from its users and the crypto community than any other cryptocurrency. It has the name recognition and principles. It still has a long way to go, but its first decade was pretty good. I believe the upcoming decade will be even better.

What makes bitcoin so great? It is decentralized and has its own blockchain. As talked about in the cryptocurrency explanation, Bitcoin has nodes all around the world and does not have a single point of failure. If one node or computer for Bitcoin shuts down, or even if several of them do, Bitcoin will continue to exist and run. Part of what makes Bitcoin valuable is that it is not restricted in any way and is accessible to all the people in the world. No government can stop its citizens from using Bitcoin. They may try to regulate it, but nobody can stop two people from agreeing to complete a transaction using Bitcoin.

CHAPTER 1: THE BASICS

Bitcoin is scarce. There are only 18,396,187 bitcoins in circulation as I write this in 2020. That is a very small amount. It has a maximum supply of 21 million. Which means no matter what, there will never be more than 21 million bitcoin in existence. In comparison, there is currently about 1.7 trillion U.S. dollars in circulation in the U.S. This scarcity of supply makes each Bitcoin more valuable as more and more people trust that Bitcoin is a real currency.

Bitcoin is apolitical. It doesn't favor a group of people or system. Bitcoin does not care if you are rich or poor, republican or democrat. It's for the people and made to help the people have control over their money.

Bitcoin is interchangeable, secure, durable, portable, non-consumable, highly divisible, programmable, and easily transacted.

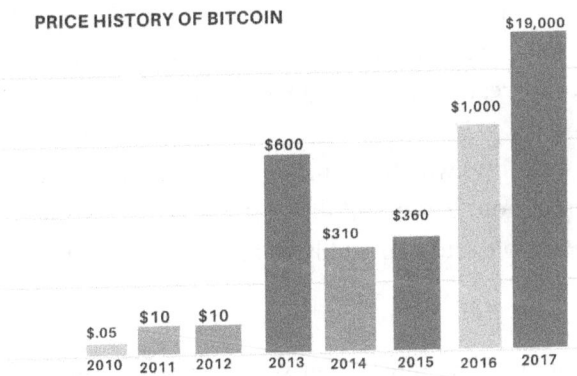

The price of Bitcoin continues to steadily increase in price over the years.

Who Is Satoshi Nakamoto?

Satoshi Nakamoto is the inventor of Bitcoin and the blockchain. But nobody knows who he or she is. Satoshi made the Bitcoin software in 2008, made it available for all in January 2009, and in 2011, disappeared. So far nobody has been able to confirm who Satoshi is. He or she is a mystery person who invented something great.

So why did Satoshi invent Bitcoin? Well the white paper for Bitcoin written by Satoshi says "What is needed is an electronic payment system based on cryptographic proof instead of trust, allowing any two willing parties to transact directly with each other without the need for a trusted third party." You have to remember what was happening in the US in 2008. Several large financial institutions failed the American people, and the country went into a recession. This recession happened because the big banks were irresponsible with our money and got greedy. In 2008, the American people didn't have much <u>trust</u> at all for banks. So Satoshi invented a trustless system called blockchain. That's why many believe that the recession in 2008 was a big reason Satoshi created Bitcoin and blockchain.

Since nobody knows who Satoshi Nakamoto is, several names have been mentioned as possibilities. Here are the names of some of the people said to possibly be Satoshi Nakamoto.

- Nick Szabo – Computer scientist and cryptographer.
- Dave Kleiman - Computer scientist and forensics expert.
- Craig Wright – Computer scientist and businessman.

- Shinichi Mochizuki – Mathematician
- Hal Finney – Computer scientist and cryptographer.
- Dorian Nakamoto – Systems and computer engineer.
- The Government – NSA (National Security Agency)

Here is the link to the Bitcoin whitepaper written by Satoshi Nakamoto. https://bitcoin.org/bitcoin.pdf

What Is a Satoshi?

A satoshi is the smallest unit of bitcoin.
 1 Satoshi = 0.00000001 bitcoin
 For example, let's say 1 bitcoin = $5,143
 If you were to buy $100 worth of bitcoin at $5,143
 $100 would = 0.01944390 bitcoin, which = 1,944,390 Satoshis.

So all you do is get rid of the leading zeros and decimal, and put commas in the appropriate places. Satoshis is how fractions of a bitcoin are expressed or written out. Instead of saying "I have 0.01944390 bitcoin." You can just say "I have 1,944,390 Satoshis."

This shows how highly divisible Bitcoin is. Especially compared to the US dollar. The smallest amount a dollar can be broken down into is one cent; $1/100^{th}$ of a dollar. But Bitcoin can be broken down to 1.0×10^{-8} or 0.00000001 bitcoin. This high divisibility is a great feature of Bitcoin. It gives the coin more flexibility in how it can be spent.

SATOSHI CONVERTER

1 Satoshi	0.00000001 BTC
10 Satoshi	0.00000010 BTC
100 Satoshi	0.00000100 BTC
1,000 Satoshi	0.00001000 BTC
10,000 Satoshi	0.00010000 BTC
100,000 Satoshi	0.00100000 BTC
1 Million Satoshi	0.01000000 BTC
10 Million Satoshi	0.10000000 BTC
100 Million Satoshi	1.00000000 BTC

Satoshis is how you express fractions of a Bitcoin.

What Are Altcoins?

An altcoin is any cryptocurrency that is not Bitcoin, and there are over 5,000 of them. Some of these altcoins are similar to Bitcoin, but many are totally different. Most are decentralized, but some aren't. Most cryptocurrencies use the blockchain to solve a problem in hopes of being used by many and changing the world. A good altcoin can help solve a problem. There are many smart people out there with experience in creating technology companies that have ideas, and use the technology of cryptocurrency and the blockchain to execute those ideas. When they do, they create a cryptocurrency that is either a token or a coin. Some popular altcoins are Ethereum, Litecoin, Cardano, EOS, Stellar, and many more.

Tokens vs Coins

Throughout this book I will use the terms coin and token depending on which cryptocurrency I am writing about. The two terms are not interchangeable. There is a big difference that is important for you to know.

A coin is any cryptocurrency that has its own blockchain. Examples of coins are Bitcoin, Ethereum, and EOS, because they interact on their own blockchain. Ethereum is the most popular coin for other cryptocurrency tokens to be built upon.

A token is any crypto that is built using an existing blockchain. Examples of tokens are Pundi X and Basic Attention Token. These tokens are built on the Ethereum blockchain. They use the platform that is Ethereum to create their token.

Ethereum is a coin and is also what we call a platform (or infrastructure coin). Other cryptocurrencies use the Ethereum platform to create their own tokens using smart contracts. The relationship is similar to a video game console and the games that work on it. Ethereum is like the PlayStation console and Pundi X (or any other token that uses Ethereum) is like the Madden game. The tokens operate using the software of Ethereum's blockchain. The same goes for other coins like EOS. Developers can use EOS's blockchain platform to create their own cryptocurrency token. Not every coin is a platform though.

To see a list of all the cryptocurrency coins and tokens, go to coinmarketcap.com. To get a good feel of how some coins can be a platform for some tokens, go to the site and click on the "Full List" of tokens. The first column will be the list of tokens, and the second column will be the coin platforms those tokens are built upon.

So if the token isn't like Bitcoin and isn't considered a currency, or isn't like Ethereum and isn't a platform, then what do you do with a token? Good question. Well, all cryptocurrencies have a price per coin/token and can be bought or sold for profit using an exchange. But a token is used to incentivize users to interact within that cryptocurrencies' ecosystem. The token can be used to get discounts within the crypto, purchase things, gain status, etc. Like how your favorite video game or app on your phone has its own native currency to incentivize you to participate or keep playing. That is what a utility token does within a crypto project.

For example, Basic Attention Token is a cryptocurrency utility token that is built on the Ethereum blockchain using smart contracts. BAT isn't meant to be spent at the local grocery store or to buy gas like a Bitcoin or Litecoin can. BAT is a digital advertising token that connects the Brave browser users, publishers, and advertisers in a decentralized way. Using the Brave browser, the user has the option to turn off ads, which can be annoying as you browse. But if you turn the ads on, users get paid in BAT tokens just to pay attention to the ads depending on how big the ad is on the page or how long it runs.

This is a great use case for a token because it makes advertising more efficient and profitable for the publisher and advertisers, and more enjoyable and profitable for the user. Also you the user can then use the BAT tokens to gain privileges within the Brave browser to have a better experience. Or you can use the BAT tokens to tip your favorite content providers on Twitter, YouTube, and Twitch, or you can send the BAT tokens to an exchange to trade it in for other cryptos, or just cash them out to get U.S. dollars.

As I write this, one BAT token is worth 23 cents. So as you collect BAT tokens browsing the internet, those tokens will become more valuable or less valuable as the years go by. But if utility tokens like BAT gain more popularity over the years and stay in business, the price per token will increase. Making your BAT tokens more valuable for you to trade for cash. Or keep them to make your internet browsing experience a great one. This is all possible due to the power of cryptocurrency, the blockchain, and smart contracts.

I know all this writing about BAT may seem like a BAT ad, but I just think it is a perfect example of a utility token and how they can be useful.

What Are Stablecoins?

A stablecoin is a cryptocurrency that is attached to another stable asset like the U.S. dollar or any other fiat. It has extremely low volatility, which means its price stays about the same, which is usually around $1. This extremely low volatility allows for the stablecoin to be used to pay for goods and services. You can be very confident that if you have $5 in a stablecoin, it will remain $5 because it is not a volatile cryptocurrency like other cryptos. Some of the most popular stablecoins are Tether, USDC, TrueUSD, and Gemini Dollar.

Cryptocurrency investors use stablecoins to protect their money from the high volatility of the cryptocurrency market. Let's say an investor purchased one bitcoin at $5,000 a coin. They will be making money as Bitcoin rises to $10,000 a coin. But what if Bitcoin drops back down from $10,000 to $7,000? The investor may want to protect the money they already made, and/or believes that the Bitcoin price will go below where he/she purchased it at $5,000. So when the Bitcoin price drops to $7,000, they decide to trade that $7,000 worth of bitcoin into Tether (USDT). Now, no matter what the cryptocurrency market does, the investors' money will stay at 7,000 Tether (USDT), which is equivalent to $7,000. The investor protected themselves from losing more money. Maybe they should have stayed patient and waited for Bitcoin to continue to rise in price. It's all up to the investor. Now the investor can keep their money in Tether until they decide to trade that Tether for another cryptocurrency, or cash out for U.S. dollars. Stablecoins are like a holding place for money so investors can make decisions on what to do next.

Or maybe the investor made a lot of money investing in a cryptocurrency and now they want to trade that crypto for U.S. dollars. But first they want to protect their money from the volatility of the market before they trade for U.S. dollars. They are done taking the risk of investing in crypto for now and want the money they made to be at a fixed amount. What a lot of investors do is trade their crypto in for a stablecoin like Tether. They turned their $1,000 into $10,000 and then they sell that crypto in exchange for Tether. They now have 10,000 USDT which is of course equal to $10,000.

Personally, I see one stablecoin eventually taking over the market. That stablecoin could be USDT, USDC, TUSD, Gemini Dollar, who knows. The people will decide. I see people owning mainly Bitcoin and possibly some other cryptocurrencies also. But cryptocurrencies are volatile, so I see an app emerging that will allow people to easily swap some Bitcoin into a stablecoin whenever they want for the purpose of spending. Remember, Bitcoin is highly divisible. Even more divisible than $1 can be broken down into cents. And I don't think the people of the world want to start re-learning how to spend their money in satoshis. The model of dollars and cents can still be maintained. So, I see an app being used that will transfer a Bitcoin's satoshis into a stablecoin's dollars and cents.

For example, let's say I want to buy a new $500 TV with some of my Bitcoin. I go online or walk inside the store and use whatever crypto swap app to transfer the satoshis that I own into 500 USDC, which is equal to $500. Or I may already have some USDC to spend. Easy.

Now, I do think that many people would like to use Bitcoin directly to buy products and services. And I think many merchants and people, if not all, will accept Bitcoin at some point in the future. It has already started. But swapping Bitcoin into a familiar fiat format will bring mass adoption faster. We can keep the dollars and cents format, just get rid of the restrictions of fiat.

I believe fiat will die to the emergence of cryptocurrencies, and stablecoins will be used often to store and spend money. The whole point of this new money system is to be more in control of what is yours and not be restricted to the limits of fiat and any limits banks put on how much we spend and when.

2

Chapter 2: SMART CONTRACTS AND MINING

What Is a Smart Contract?

A smart contract is a computer protocol on the blockchain that can self-execute the terms of an agreement without the need of a middleman. The details of the agreement are written into lines of code. A smart contract can help you exchange anything of value like money, property, or information without any conflict with the other person because all the terms are executed using the If-Then premise on the blockchain. It is a faster and cheaper way to execute transactions.

The ability to execute transactions on the blockchain without a middleman was done first using Bitcoin. But Bitcoin is limited to transacting bitcoin only. The smart contract allows developers to write their own lines of code to be able to transfer anything of value on the blockchain. This is done using the

Ethereum software. Ethereum is the #2 cryptocurrency right now right behind Bitcoin. Developers use Ethereum software to program their own smart contracts. So while Bitcoin just transacts bitcoin on the blockchain, Ethereum is a software that allows anything of value to be transacted on the blockchain.

The smart contract has been described as a digital vending machine. You put something of value in and you get an item of value in return. All of this gets done without having to fill out forms that could take a lot of time and possibly have errors. With smart contracts you save time because you don't have to wait on the middleman like a lawyer or broker to confirm anything. Plus the smart contract is not biased towards either party, and it won't commit errors. All parties can trust the smart contract to execute on time. And since this all occurs on the blockchain, everything involved in the transaction is duplicated on all of the nodes, so everything is automatically backed up.

Smart contract technology can change the game because it can be used in so many different situations and in so many different industries. This technology can be used in real estate, health care system, government, supply chain, and many other areas of business in everyday life.

Here is a real world example of how a smart contract works. Let's say there is a smart contract with lines of code programmed to execute renting storage space from a local storage company. You pay in cryptocurrency on the blockchain and get a receipt within the contract, and the storage company gives you a storage combination to the lock, which should be given to you by a certain time and date. If you don't get it by a certain time and date, the smart contract will give you a refund. If the storage company does give the combination to you before it is due, the crypto you paid and the combination they gave will be held within the contract until the agreed upon time. Then they get the crypto payment and you get the combination. If the storage company tries to change anything in the smart contract code, it cannot be done without you knowing about it. Everybody gets what they need. No fraud. Both you and the storage company trusted the transaction to be executed correctly while you were running another errand or relaxing at home.

You may be thinking, well I could do all of this by calling the storage company or going to the location myself. You could, but would the process be as easy, hassle free, or stress free? Because during the process you both can trust the smart contract to execute every step without worrying about if it's done right, what's next, or if you're getting cheated. If somebody doesn't provide the right information or money on time, the smart contract handles that automatically. You trust the smart contract to get it right for everybody. So when the transaction is over, both parties will know everything went well.

There is a cryptocurrency token called Power Ledger that uses the Ethereum smart contract on the blockchain to trade excess energy between two parties. A person with a solar panel on their roof can use it to sell excess energy to their neighbor. There are many different use cases for smart contracts.

It may seem to you that there are a lot of jobs being replaced by the blockchain and smart contracts. But actually, professionals in all industries will still be needed. It is just that when it is time to exchange data and value, the smart contract on the blockchain can execute it better. All parties involved including the broker, real estate agent, lawyer, etc., can benefit from the time being saved and easy execution of the transaction with way less paperwork and errors. These jobs in all industries bring much value in making the world go around. Smart contracts just make it go smoother.

What Is Mining?

Mining is the process in which transactions of a cryptocurrency are verified and added to the blockchain using computers (nodes). These computers compete with other computers to solve the next block using cryptography. Once the block is solved, the transaction is permanently added to the blockchain and the miner who solved the problem is rewarded with that cryptocurrency. This reward of getting paid in the crypto you are mining is the great incentive that keeps the blockchain going. Nobody works for free.

Mining is essential for the blockchain to work. The computers or nodes that mine cryptocurrency are all one part of the process that allows transactions on the blockchain to occur without a third party. Computers that mine verify the transactions, make sure the transaction isn't false, and keep the blockchain running.

Mining cryptocurrencies like Bitcoin require powerful computers that take up a lot of electricity. There is another mining method that does not need powerful computers to mine, but I will get into that soon.

So basically, a person decides they want to earn some cryptocurrency by mining cryptocurrency. The miner then buys and sets up a powerful computer to mine that cryptocurrency. Then they find and download the correct mining software for that cryptocurrency. These powerful mining computers compete with other powerful mining computers to solve a complicated encrypted block. That complicated encrypted block represents a transaction between two people, like one person sending Bitcoin to another. The computers solve the encrypted block and add it to the blockchain. The transaction between the two people is now complete. The miner is rewarded with that blockchain's crypto depending on how much their computer contributed to solving the encrypted block. That is mining!

Mining can be very profitable. It must be profitable for the person mining, or else they wouldn't do it and there would be no computers or nodes to make new blocks on the blockchain. As I write this book, there are over 10,000 reachable Bitcoin nodes all over the world. 19% of them are in the USA as of now. The more nodes there are, the more unstoppable Bitcoin will be. The same goes for other cryptocurrencies on their blockchain.

What Is Proof of Work (PoW)?

There are two main methods used to mine cryptocurrencies. The first one used is called proof of work. It is the method discussed in the previous section about mining. Bitcoin is mined using the proof of work method. Proof of Work is the original consensus algorithm used in a blockchain network. With Proof of Work, the miners need very powerful computers that use large amounts of electricity. The miners with the most powerful computers get the first opportunities to confirm transactions and create new blocks. Once the computer mines the crypto, they get rewarded with some of the crypto coins or tokens.

There are also large warehouses full of powerful computers all around the world that are there just to mine Bitcoin using the Proof of Work method. The downside to Proof of Work is that it uses an incredibly high amount of electricity and its dependence on specialized hardware can prevent necessary growth. Most people wont buy a high powered computer and start running a high electricity bill to mine anything.

What Is Proof of Stake (PoS)?

The other method of mining cryptocurrency is Proof of Stake. Proof of Stake is a randomized system in which the creator or validator of the next block is based upon how much of that cryptocurrency the user is holding, the length of time the user has been holding it, and other randomization factors. In PoS, the term forged is used instead of mine. The more crypto you hold, the higher your chances of being randomly chosen to create the next block and be rewarded with some of that crypto. This method encourages owners of a crypto to hold their coins/tokens for a long period of time on that cryptocurrencies network. The fact that proof of stake has a randomization factor promotes the idea of decentralization. Even the richest person who owns the most amount of that cryptocurrency will not be the only one receiving staking rewards because the randomization will allow users holding smaller amounts to receive staking rewards also.

For example, lets say a cryptocurrency has 100 tokens in circulation. Dominic holds 50 tokens, Deion holds 25 tokens, Latoya holds 15 tokens, and Xavier holds 10 tokens. Dominic has a greater chance than everybody else to be selected to validate the next block because he has more tokens staked than everybody else. But remember there are other randomization factors involved in choosing the next forger. Even though Xavier has the least amount of tokens staked (10), lets say he has had those tokens staked the longest out of the other 3 forgers. That age factor will help Xavier be chosen to forge the next block more often. So, even though Dominic holds the most tokens and has a greater chance of being chosen to forge the next block, due to randomization, he will still not be chosen all the time to receive rewards. Leaving Deion, Latoya, and Xavier with good chances to forge the next block and regularly receive some staking rewards.

The upside to Proof of Stake is that it does not use nearly the amount of electricity Proof of Work does. Because of this, more users will be capable of participating in the Proof of Stake forging method. With Proof of Stake, you only need to send your cryptocurrency to a certain website and follow detailed instructions in order to stake your coins/tokens. All you need is a regular computer, and in some cases a smart phone. Much easier than setting up a high powered computer.

If you want to be a forger using the Proof of Stake method, do research on the cryptocurrency you would like to forge; and if Proof of Stake is their method of validating their next block, you will find instructions on how to participate. You stake your crypto and help forge their crypto on the blockchain, they reward you with some of that crypto. It's a win-win relationship.

Proof of Stake is a great way to make passive income. All you do is stake your crypto, let it sit, and earn rewards without you having to do anymore work. It's like earning interest on a traditional investment except there is no risk. The crypto you earned staking, you got for free, so if the price of that crypto goes down, oh well. If the price goes up, you made free money. The interest rates in PoS are much higher than any bank savings account, and the crypto you earn as rewards has the potential to go up in value. The US dollars you earn in a traditional investment or in a bank savings account don't go up in value. If you earn $1 in interest from a traditional investment, it will always be $1. But if you earn one token of staking rewards at 4 cents a token for example, that crypto token can decrease in value or be worth way more than 4 cents one day. Therefore multiplying your investment

Just so you can see how real Proof of Stake is, the picture below is a screenshot of the Cardano (ADA) that I currently have staked. As you can see I staked 10,767 ADA coins originally and have been rewarded with 421 ADA coins so far. All I did was follow the simple instructions to stake my coins and just let it sit. I get rewarded with some ADA every one to two days depending on how much my staked coins were involved in forging the next ADA block. The longer I keep my ADA staked, the more rewards I will get once I forge. See, it's real!

The total of ADA I staked, the rewards I have received so far, and the total of it all.

3

Chapter 3: CRYPTO AND FIAT MENTALITIES

Different Mentalities

Just so you know, just like everything else in life, people within the cryptocurrency community have many different opinions on the future of crypto. I just want to inform you of the two major frames of thought out there. On one side you have the Bitcoin maximalists, and on the other, the people who believe in Bitcoin and also believe in some altcoins.

Bitcoin maximalist believe that Bitcoin is the only cryptocurrency that will last the test of time. They believe that even if some altcoins have good use cases they are not good enough to last and be adopted by the masses. They only believe in Bitcoin and will only buy Bitcoin.

The people who believe in Bitcoin and some altcoins believe in Bitcoin just like the maximalists do, but they believe that some altcoins have really good use cases and that some of them will last the test of time. They may own some Bitcoin or no Bitcoin, but their portfolio definitely has some altcoins in it.

One of the main reasons people believe in altcoins is the fact that altcoins bring more multipliers. By multipliers I mean the number of times an investment can multiply your money. Which means you can make more money faster investing in altcoins than you can with Bitcoin. An altcoin can multiply your money by 10x, 50x, 100x, 200x plus depending on what you buy, when you buy, and when you cash out. But the downside is that some altcoins will not increase in price at all, or increase very little, or look promising at first and have a lot of hype before failing, because a lot of them aren't as reliable or get enough attention. Bitcoin may not bring the great multipliers that altcoins do, but at this point Bitcoin can still multiply 10x or more depending on when you buy and how long you hold. You can definitely make more money quicker with the right altcoin, but Bitcoin is a more reliable investment.

Bitcoin just won't multiply as many times to make you as much money. Why? Because the Bitcoin price is already so high. The higher the price of a crypto when you buy it, the lower your chances of it multiplying as many times to make your money grow. As I write this chapter, Bitcoin is about $9,500 per coin. If you buy at this price, the price must go to $19,000 a coin for you to double your money. But if you buy an altcoin at 1 cent a coin/token, the price only has to go to 2 cents for your money to double. The lower a number, the quicker it will multiply. The higher a number, the longer it will take to multiply.

Bitcoin is more reliable and a better store of value. It has proven that it always recovers and reaches higher highs. So like everything else in life, you look at the pros and cons and make your decision. Personally, I own both because I believe in Bitcoin and certain altcoins.

How Money is Trusted as an Exchange of Value

You may be thinking, "How does a Bitcoin or any other cryptocurrency have any value?" "I mean, I can't even touch it." That is a good question. But you then must ask yourself the same question when it comes to the U.S. dollar, Euro, or any other form of fiat used today. The reason a $10 bill can be used to buy a product is because we (country, world) believe that the $10 bill has the value that is printed on it. We all have trust in it. We all believe in it. We trust that someone else will also believe in its value and take it in exchange for goods and services. A $1 bill is printed on the same paper as a $100 bill (75% cotton and 25% linen), but a $100 bill is 100 times more valuable than the $1 bill. Why? Because all of us believe that the $100 bill is more valuable and can trust that someone else will also believe the $100 bill is more valuable than the $1 bill.

Any society at any point in time can create value in anything, if the people trust in its value together. A pencil could be used as currency. I know. That sounds stupid but apply the same concept from earlier. If the USA as a whole believed and trusted that a single wooden pencil was worth something that could be agreed upon, then wooden pencils would be used to buy goods and services. Value can be placed on anything. Of course, it also helps if there is something unique that can cause and create value in a thing. For cryptocurrency, those unique attributes are the blockchain, smart contracts on the blockchain, the idea of decentralization, trustless transactions, etc. These principles I just listed are way more valuable than just a form of currency that we are all used to using and have believed in for no other reason than it is what we all like to use. Therefore, cryptocurrency is more valuable and has a lot more to offer than fiat. The only thing you can do with a dollar bill is earn it and spend it. You can earn and spend cryptocurrency and use the blockchain to transact anything. The U.S. dollar didn't come with its own technology, but cryptocurrency does. The blockchain.

We are at the very beginning of a new financial and technological revolution. Most people aren't living during a major change in what we use as money. You are! That's exciting!

In the history of the world, the bartering system, food, stones, shells, precious metals, and paper have been used as currency. At some point society moves on from one to the next. It may take some time to be fully adopted by the people, but there will always be change.

Right now, paper money (fiat) is the main form of currency. Credit cards, debit cards, and checks, are all based on the value of paper money and coins. Your money can be represented in a physical form; paper money, or it can be represented in a digital form; credit and debit. Most people get paid by direct deposit or check. A lot of people spend most of their money using debit and credit cards without even seeing the paper money they own that backs it up. People have already been getting accustomed to owning money, but never seeing it physically. So naturally, the next step is to get rid of the paper money and coins completely and go all digital. With cryptocurrency the power is put in the people's hands. It has already started.

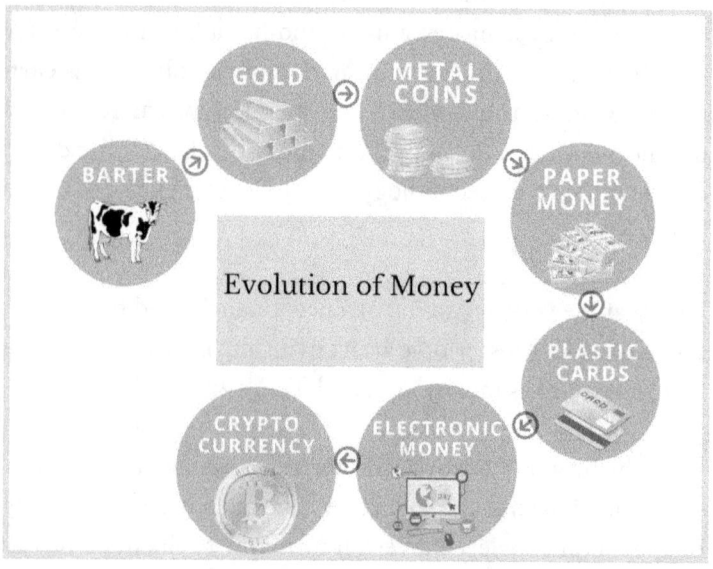

The money we use will evolve over time. Cryptocurrency is next.

Go to coinmarketcap.com. See the value being placed on all those cryptocurrencies. Some will die off soon and some will be around for a long time. As for Bitcoin, there are already millions of people that trust in it and believe in its value. Even though those people are currently in the minority, that is okay because it is still very early. They believe that a digital coin that they can't touch, that is just a long series of letters and numbers, has value. They are already exchanging their paper money for it and buying food, cars, houses, etc. with it. Now all that needs to happen is what we call "mass adoption". That is when more and more people of the world believe, trust, and use Bitcoin and other cryptocurrencies also.

Many investors are investing in cryptocurrency in order to gain more fiat. They buy a cryptocurrency using fiat, see the coin/token increase in price, and then sell it to make a profit in fiat. Even though you may want to do the same, you may be wondering if cryptocurrency enthusiasts believe in it so much, why then cash out their crypto for more fiat? The reason is that fiat is still the more widely accepted form of currency. Fiat is needed to exchange for goods and services way more than cryptocurrency is right now. But we believe that will change.

The strategy of many cryptocurrency investors is to also buy Bitcoin and never cash it out for fiat. To accumulate more Bitcoin so that if it becomes the main form of currency, they will already have at least some fractions of Bitcoin to buy goods and services with. Because they believe that fiat will eventually fade away and the world will adopt some cryptocurrencies, mainly Bitcoin because of the trust it has gained and the belief that many will have in it. So even though crypto can make a person more fiat, it is also a smart strategy to accumulate Bitcoin and some altcoins for future use.

4

Chapter 4: BUYING AND SELLING

Buying and Selling

The process of buying and selling most cryptocurrencies is more complicated than it should be. It is one of the things standing in the way of mass adoption. Buying and selling more cryptocurrencies must be easier to understand and execute in order for more people to participate.

But there are two easy ways to buy the top coins/tokens. That is with the Voyager app and Coinbase. There are other apps like Robinhood or the Cash app that allow you to buy Bitcoin. But with Coinbase and the Voyager app you can buy the top cryptocurrencies using your credit/debit card or bank account (fiat). With these platforms, buying cryptocurrency is as easy as shopping online.

Coinbase is an exchange that came along first and is very popular in the crypto community. Its website interface is easy to navigate and there is also a Coinbase app. Coinbase charges a small fee when you are buying crypto with your fiat. The fee is higher when using your credit/debit card, and lower when using your bank account. The Voyager app is a crypto trading app. It is newer and right now has more coins/tokens available to buy than Coinbase. The great thing about Voyager is that there are no fees on trades. I suggest you download both and figure out which one is your favorite. These two trading platforms will be the very beginning of your crypto buying journey.

Trading Pairs

While you can buy some of the top cryptocurrencies with fiat using Coinbase and Voyager, most coins/tokens can only be purchased using another cryptocurrency. So that means you have to buy one crypto using fiat on Coinbase or Voyager, then use that crypto to buy the one you ultimately want, using what is called a trading pair.

A trading pair is the relationship between a pair of cryptocurrencies showing that one is used to buy another. For example, ADA/BTC is a trading pair. This means you can use Bitcoin (BTC) to buy Cardano (ADA). The crypto listed first is the one you want to buy, and the crypto listed second is the one needed to buy the first crypto. When you are on a cryptocurrency exchange, you will see several trading pairs. Some cryptocurrencies only have one, some have many. Bitcoin and Ethereum are the most popular coins used to buy other cryptocurrencies. You can buy some cryptos with both Bitcoin and Ethereum. Stablecoins like Tether (USDT) and USD Coin

(USDC) are also often used in trading pairs.

Common Buying Scenario

Let's say you want to buy Power Ledger (POWR) tokens. You've done your research and you are ready to invest in Power Ledger. Right now, like many cryptocurrencies, you cannot buy Power Ledger tokens on Coinbase or Voyager with US dollars. You can only buy Power Ledger (POWR) using Bitcoin (BTC), Ethereum (ETH), Tether (USDT), USD Coin (USDC), and some others on an exchange. So what you have to do is go to an exchange where you want to buy Power Ledger and see which trading pairs are available to buy Power Ledger. Let's say you go to the exchange that has Power Ledger and see it has POWR/ETH, POWR/BTC, and POWR/USDT trading pairs. And you decide you want to buy Power Ledger using the POWR/ETH trading pair. So now you know you need Ethereum to buy Power Ledger. So first you must buy Ethereum. You go to an exchange like Coinbase or Voyager that lets you use US dollars to buy certain cryptocurrencies and buy some Ethereum (ETH). You then send the ETH to the exchange that has Power Ledger. Once the ETH shows up in your account on that exchange, you find the trading pair of POWR/ETH and use your Ethereum (ETH) to buy Power Ledger (POWR). Now you are the proud owner of Power Ledger.

This buying process may seem unnecessarily complicated at first. But once you do it a couple times, it won't seem complicated at all.

It is still the wild wild west in the world of cryptocurrency, and there are still some processes that need to be simplified. But as mass adoption increases, buying cryptocurrencies will be much easier.

Exchanges

Cryptocurrency exchanges are websites and apps where you can buy cryptocurrency using U.S. dollars or other cryptocurrencies. The idea is that if you want a certain coin/token, you must go to an exchange to get it. Just like many sites, you must create a profile in order to use it. But not all exchanges are equal. Some are not as trustworthy as others. Some exchanges lie about the amount of money spent on their platform a day. This is referred to as 24 hour volume. Avoid any exchange with a bad reputation.

The more popular the exchange, the more reliable it is for the most part. See where other cryptocurrency investors are buying their crypto and their experiences with that site. Twitter and Telegram are very useful in seeing the experiences of other crypto investors.

Sometimes a great exchange with a great reputation may not have the coin/token you want, and a less popular exchange does. Go ahead and get the coin/token from that lesser known exchange, but make sure you withdraw your crypto as soon as you buy it and send it to your wallet. That goes for all exchanges.

Security on Exchanges

Never keep your crypto on the exchange after you buy it unless you plan on trading that crypto very soon. Otherwise, get your crypto off the exchange by sending it to your wallet. Why? Because exchanges have been known to be hacked, and you don't want to have your investment stolen because some evil hacker stole millions of dollars of crypto from an exchange, and you were one of the victims. There is a famous saying in the crypto community. "Not your keys, not your crypto." Which means if your crypto is not stored in a wallet that you have the private keys to, then it is not your crypto, because you really don't have possession of it. You are the best person to possess and keep your cryptocurrency safe.

Where to Buy Your Crypto

A good way to know what exchange sells the coin/token you want to buy is the website coinmarketcap.com. This site lists all 5,000 plus cryptocurrencies along with their current and past price, market cap, 24 hour volume, and many other data points. One of the most useful data points on the site is that you can find the coin/token you are interested in and find all the exchanges that are selling it. Just click on or search for the coin/token, then click on the "Market Pairs" tab and you will see every exchange selling that crypto in order of 24 hour volume. 24 hour volume is the total amount in US dollars traded in the last 24 hours to buy or sell a cryptocurrency. Usually the exchanges with the highest 24 hour volume are the most reliable exchanges to buy or sell your cryptocurrency. Click on the exchanges to get more information on them, including a link to the exchange itself. Coinmarketcap.com is one of the most popular and useful sites for anybody in the cryptocurrency space.

Withdrawal Fees

Once you have purchased a coin/token from an exchange, you now want to send it to your wallet address; unless you are doing some trading of course. In that case, you keep your crypto on the exchange to trade. But if not trading, withdraw your crypto ASAP. When you withdraw the crypto from the exchange, there will be a fee. The fee is usually, if not always, a portion of the cryptocurrency you just purchased. For example, you may have just bought 100 Cardano (ADA). The fee to withdraw the ADA from that exchange could be 1 ADA. So when you receive the ADA in your wallet, you will get 99 ADA. These fees can vary depending on the state of the market, which coin/token you are withdrawing, and the exchange you are withdrawing from. Some cryptos have larger fees than others, but every exchange is different.

You can see what the withdrawal fees are for each cryptocurrency from some exchanges by going to the coin/token you are interested in on that exchange and clicking on the withdrawal section to see the fee. You may see that one exchange charges less than another. I just don't want you to be surprised by the fees when you withdraw your crypto. But most of the fees I have seen are very minimal. Definitely way less than any fees a bank would charge you to wire money.

Decentralized Exchanges

Decentralized exchanges are exchanges that allow you to connect your wallet directly to an exchange, buy your crypto, and then store the crypto directly on your wallet. So instead of trusting an exchange with your cryptocurrency to buy more cryptocurrency, a decentralized exchange allows you to plug your crypto from your wallet directly into the exchange, use the crypto funds in your wallet to buy more crypto, and store it directly back into your wallet without having to withdraw or leaving your newly purchased crypto on the exchange for it to be potentially hacked. And you are exchanging directly with other users (peer-to-peer). There is no third party to hold the funds.

At first using a decentralized exchange was intimidating for me. The websites are not as user friendly and they look real technical compared to regular crypto exchanges. Well at least the ones I used. But once I figured it out, it was the best cryptocurrency buying experience. Why? Because it really gets you connected to one of the core principles of cryptocurrency, decentralization. The peer-to-peer interaction is also a huge part of the great experience. Being able to plug in my cold storage wallet (see next chapter) via USB and buy crypto from a peer online directly is extremely satisfying and the way exchanges of money and other things of value should be executed. It is very similar to downloading music on peer-to-peer sites like Napster back in the day. Except decentralized exchanges are legal, the cryptocurrency I "downloaded" is legally mine, and it has the potential to be way more valuable than an MP3.

5

Chapter 5: STORING YOUR CRYPTOCURRENCY

Storing Your Cryptocurrency

How and where you store your cryptocurrency is the most important decision you will make in your crypto investing. Why? Because it doesn't matter if you make a great investment in a successful cryptocurrency. Or if you make a horrible investment in a scam coin. If you lose your private keys, or passphrases, or store them in a place where they can be hacked, you could possibly loose it all. You need to store your cryptocurrency in very reliable places with backups.

I know all of that sounds scary, but in this cryptocurrency world you are responsible for your own crypto. Remember this is decentralization. There is no big bank where you can store your crypto. If a bank gets robbed of all its money, you will get your money back because it is FDIC insured up to 250k. Most people have a history with banks and feel confident that their money is safe there. But the banks can restrict you from getting to your money. They control how you get it, control when you can get it, charge you unnecessary fees, and you are susceptible to their websites/systems crashing. They are a single point of failure.

Wells Fargo had their websites go down for over a day one time in 2019 because they had a fire in one of their facilities. None of their customers could login to the website or mobile app to access their funds for about a day. And the debit cards didn't work. You really aren't in control of your money. Plus, you have restrictions on how much you can spend from your debit card in a day, how much cash you can withdraw in a day, how many times you can withdraw from your savings account a month, fees, banking hours, etc. You are just used to the process of storing and retrieving your money in the bank. I banked at Wells Fargo. I work hard. And because they had a single point of failure, (the building that had a fire and smoke that caused the system to shutdown) I couldn't use my debit card, move my money around, send money, or anything. I didn't have access to my own money! That's crazy. With cryptocurrency, you don't rely on a middle man or third party, you rely on yourself. You rely on the blockchain. That may be scary to some of you all. It was scary to me at first, but it is better that the power over your money be in your hands.

Surface Level: Wallets, Private Keys, Public Addresses

Before you buy your cryptocurrency, first figure out what kind of wallet you want to store it in. You then send it to your cryptocurrency wallet address. You will also get a private key (that you should never share with anybody) that gives yourself access to your cryptocurrency. Then you will get your recovery passphrase that will allow you to recover your cryptocurrency in case you ever lose your private keys. Now here are the definitions of wallet, public address, private keys, and recovery passphrase.

Wallet – a software program that stores private and public keys and enables you to send and receive cryptocurrency by interacting with multiple blockchains.

Public Address – A string of alphanumeric characters that is used in sending and receiving cryptocurrency. To receive cryptocurrency, you need to give the sender your address. To send cryptocurrency, you need to know what address to send it to. Ex: 1J43GSWSiepsGjPnmQ8g6Ueuutkfs1zOBd

Private Keys – A string of alphanumeric characters that gives you access to your cryptocurrency and allows you to send your cryptocurrency to others. If it is lost, you can't send your crypto. Ex: Bi568JieDer671QWV97KLhu0924HbN-MLPPI871Q3r6YuiNaqqZxFGjl9478lkmm1

Recovery Passphrase – A list of 12-24 random words that is given to you once you create a wallet. It will allow you to recover your cryptocurrency if you ever forget or are not able to access your private keys.

A Little Deeper: Wallets

There are five types of wallets. Hardware, mobile, desktop, paper, and online.

Hardware – a wallet that is a secure USB type device that can be plugged into any computer. It is not connected to the internet. Also referred to as "cold" storage. The most secure way to store your cryptocurrency.

Mobile – a wallet kept on your mobile phone. It comes in the form of an app that you can download.

Desktop – a wallet kept on your desktop or laptop computer. It can be downloaded from websites.

Paper – a wallet where the private keys and public address is written or typed on a piece of paper. It is one of the more secure wallets because it is never connected to the internet. It is also known as a form of "cold" storage.

Online – a wallet created on a cryptocurrency wallet website.

Once you have decided what type of wallet you want to use, do all the setup that it takes to create a username and password. Then you will be asked to write down the recovery passphrases. Get a pen and paper and write down these random words right away in the order you see them in. This recovery passphrase will be the only way you can recover your cryptocurrency if you lose your wallet and can't access your private keys.

Then you should see your wallet public address. Go to wherever your cryptocurrency is stored and go to the withdrawal section. Copy and paste your wallet address into the withdrawal section because you want to withdraw your crypto from there to your new wallet. There are usually QR codes available for you to scan if you can also. This will help prevent any errors in copying and pasting. Then check and make sure the address pasted in the withdrawal section of wherever your crypto is currently stored matches your wallet address.

Now you only want to send a small amount first because you want to make sure your cryptocurrency is sent successfully to your wallet address. If for any reason you copied wrong or made a mistake in entering your wallet address, you will lose your crypto. You don't want that to happen, so send a very small amount first. You can google "[cryptocurrency you have] blockchain explorer" to track the status of the crypto you just sent. We will get into that more later in this chapter.

Once you see that your cryptocurrency has arrived safely to your wallet, go ahead and send the rest using the same process. Now your cryptocurrency is safe in your own personal wallet. You now own your own private keys. Congratulations. You have put yourself in the best position to keep your cryptocurrency safe.

Sending Crypto

Now if you want to send your cryptocurrency from your wallet to anywhere else like an exchange or another wallet, click "Send" or "Withdraw" in your wallet. Paste or scan the destination address and enter the amount you want to send. You can also send a small amount first if you would like to make sure you're sending to the correct destination. And you can check a blockchain explorer to track the status.

Now remember you need your private keys in order to send your cryptocurrency from your wallet. If you are using a paper wallet, you will have to manually enter or scan a QR code of your private keys in order to send your crypto. But if you are using a hardware, online, desktop, or mobile wallet you have already accessed your private keys once you have logged in with your username and password or pin. You don't have to type it in with those wallets. Some digital wallets may ask you to re-enter your pin or password for confirmation before sending. Now your crypto has been sent.

A Little Deeper: Private Keys and Public Addresses

Your wallet doesn't actually hold your cryptocurrency. It only holds your private keys and public address. Your cryptocurrency stays stored on the blockchain. Your address tells everyone where your crypto is located on the blockchain. Just like your home address let's everyone know where you live. Your wallet address can be shared with anybody. Other people will not have access to your cryptocurrency if they have your wallet address. All they can do is send you more crypto.

Your private keys allow you to access your crypto in order to send it to others. Your cryptocurrency can not be sent from your wallet if your private keys are not given or confirmed. If the public address lets everyone know where your crypto is housed on the blockchain, the private keys are the "keys" to opening the door and getting access to your crypto on the blockchain. Never share your private keys. If somebody gets access to your private keys, they have access to your cryptocurrency.

Backing Up Private Keys, Public Address, Password, and Recovery Passphrases

Now that you have your wallet setup with a public address, private key, password, and recovery passphrases, you now want to back all this information up. Imagine you lose your paper wallet, or you lose your phone with your mobile wallet on it, or your house burns down and your hardware wallet or computer burns up. These are common and extreme events, but they can all happen. And if they do happen and you didn't back up your recovery passphrase, you will never be able to access your crypto again. It is all lost. There is no 1-800 number to call. That is it! Follow these easy steps to back up your cryptocurrency recovery words.

1. When creating a wallet, write down the recovery passphrases on a piece of paper. Make copies of that paper.

2. On your computer, open Notes or a word processor and type the recovery words in the same order you wrote it down on the paper.
3. Get a couple of USB drives (as many as you want) and save those recovery words on the USB drives.
4. You can save wallet passwords, usernames, private keys, public addresses, or any other details you want along with your recovery passphrases on the USB drives.
5. Do not save the recovery passphrases on your computer, don't email it to yourself or anybody else, and don't save it on the cloud. Only save it on the USB drive. This will allow your recovery passphrases to be safe from anybody hacking your computer, email, or cloud service.
6. Store the pieces of paper and the USB drives with the recovery passphrases in safe places. Wherever you consider safe is good. A safe, a drawer not used by anybody but you, hidden compartments, etc.
7. Last, give a USB drive to a couple people you trust in your life. Somebody who won't steal your cryptocurrency, somebody who has your best interests at heart. Just in case something happens to your copies, they can back you up.

Blockchain Explorer

A blockchain explorer or block explorer is a search tool for blockchains. You use a block explorer just like you would use Google to search the internet. Except here, you are using the block explorer to search the blockchain. Remember, a blockchain is a trusted network of computers called nodes that all have the same history of transactions. The blockchain for most cryptocurrencies is public information. On the block explorer you can check your wallet balance just by entering your wallet's public address, see the status of a transaction, and check pretty much any transaction details on the blockchain.

Now each coin that has its own blockchain will have its own block explorer. For example Bitcoin has its own block explorer, Cardano has its own block explorer, and any token that is built on the Ethereum platform can be searched on the Ethereum block explorer (www.etherscan.io). Just google the cryptocurrency you want to explore and the words "block explorer" and the appropriate block explorer should be in the top results.

So after you send a cryptocurrency to another address, you can then go to the appropriate block explorer site, enter the address you sent it to or the hash number, and you will be able to see the status of the crypto you sent. You will be able to see the confirmations as they occur. This can ease your mind if you are ever concerned about the length of time it is taking for your crypto to arrive to another address.

6

Chapter 6: ADVICE

Advice, But Not Financial Advice

Take your time when sending and receiving cryptocurrency. In crypto, anybody whether it is an exchange, a merchant, or another person, has a deposit address for each cryptocurrency. This address is a long unique series of numbers and letters that serves as a location to send and receive cryptocurrency.

When you are sending cryptocurrency anywhere, you will need to know the receivers deposit address. You will have to copy this address on your computer or phone and paste it into the deposit address field. Sometimes a QR Code is given so you can scan it with your phone and the address will appear without you having to type it out or copy. But this is very important. This is one reason why cryptocurrency is still the Wild Wild West. If you make a mistake and enter the wrong address, or send a crypto to the wrong address, like for example, sending

Bitcoin to an Ethereum address, your cryptocurrency will be lost forever! That is why you better be very careful when sending cryptocurrency anywhere. It can be nerve racking but here are some simple tips.

First, make sure you are sending the cryptocurrency to the specific address that is set up for that particular cryptocurrency. Only send Bitcoin to a Bitcoin address and only send XRP to an XRP address. Each exchange or person you are sending to has a designated address for each crypto or each kind of crypto.

If you do scan the deposit address QR code, still verify the address letter by letter and number by number before you send. If you simply copy and paste the address, make sure you have copied the whole address and pasted it completely. Then check the address for accuracy.

Once you do that, (I stated this before, but this is very important) I recommend you only send a small amount of cryptocurrency to the deposit address first. This way you make sure the crypto was sent to the correct address successfully. And if you made a mistake in copying, or sent the crypto to the wrong address, you will have not lost a large amount of your crypto. If the small amount you sent made it to the address successfully, then you have the confidence to send your remaining crypto. Now there are some blockchain services that make addresses easier to identify and help prevent mistakes, but this is the basic way to send cryptocurrency.

Don't let this scare you. We are so used to relying on banks for these types of transactions. We are used to knowing that if something goes wrong, we can get help from the bank. But remember, one of the biggest reasons for cryptocurrency and blockchain technology is to avoid these big banks. To be decentralized. So, embrace the intense responsibility of being the sole owner of your cryptocurrency. It is the future.

Do Your Own Research

As you get more into the world of cryptocurrency, you will see that there are over 5,000 crypto projects out there. Too many to keep up with. You may want to get some expert opinions on what to invest in and why. See what is hot in the crypto world. It is a good idea to get connected to the crypto community through social media. Especially on YouTube, Twitter, Telegram, Instagram, and Redditt. As you look, you will find some online personalities that you like and learn to trust. A lot of these people work hard to give you well-sourced news and educated opinions and guesses. But as you decide what you want to buy, you need to make sure you Do Your Own Research (DYOR)!

I recommend that you vet these crypto enthusiasts very carefully. There are a lot of people talking about many cryptocurrencies and you need to make sure they are people you can trust. Here is what I recommend you think about or ask yourself.

- Gauge their intentions. Why are they sharing information or their opinion?
- How are they qualified to be a trusted source?
- Have they scammed people in the past?

- How do they make money? When you understand how people make money, it can help you gauge how genuine they are in sharing good information with you, the viewer.
- Do they seem like they care about the crypto community?

It is a good idea to see what others think about certain cryptos you are interested in. Especially since you do want to invest in something that other investors also think is a good project. There are plenty of great YouTubers and other social media enthusiasts; but the ultimate decision on what to do with your money is up to you. Don't invest in a crypto blindly just because somebody else said it would make you a lot of money. DYOR!

So after you watch the YouTube video or read the article, or tweet, or Redditt post that hyped you up about a crypto, here is what you need to do.

- **Go to the crypto project's website** – see if the website is legit. Does it tell the visitor about the project? See if it is a site that you think somebody would make if they were serious about creating a successful business. Did they put effort into making it user friendly?

- **Read the white paper** – A white paper is an official document written by a new cryptocurrency project outlining the problem they want to solve, the methodology to solve the problem, a description of the product, and how it will interact with the users. It can be long and boring sometimes, but it is good to read. Just make sure you have a good understanding of what the team for the project wants to do and if you think it is worth investing your money. It should be on their website.

- **Find the Roadmap** – A roadmap is a laid out plan of what goals the crypto project plans to reach each quarter for the current year and maybe a year or two out. You can find it on their website. See if they are planning to accomplish goals consistently throughout the year to grow and develop the project. Also see if they have accomplished past goals. These accomplished goals could help add value to the crypto over time.

- **Team** – How experienced are the members of the team when it comes to business, cryptocurrency, blockchain technology; and have they been successful in their previous businesses. Sometimes if the CEO and the team surrounding them have great experience in the previously mentioned fields, it can bring a lot of excitement and positive hype to that project. The team is usually at the bottom of the crypto project's website.

- **Social media following** – Are there other investors excited about this project and talking about it on social media platforms? Do they have a great following that believes in it, supports each other in the good and bad times, and bring perceived value to the crypto in the eyes of potential investors?

- **Are they sharing information?** – Is the project letting their investors know what they are working on and what to expect next? Or are they too quiet for too long without any updates? Are they creative with the sharing of their information? Twitter, Telegram, and YouTube are the main social media platforms crypto projects use to communicate. The project you are investing in should have at least a Twitter and Telegram account.

- **What is the use case?** - What is the purpose of this cryptocurrency? What problem does it solve? Is there another crypto doing the same but better or worse? Make sure you understand what this project is trying to accomplish and that you believe that the project will be successful.

- **Do they have a good marketing team?** – Now this is the least important, because there are some great projects out there that don't have the best marketing plan. But it would be nice if the crypto project did a great job of letting the crypto community and the world know what they are doing consistently and in a unique way to get quality attention.

After you have done these things, you can know that the decision to invest in a cryptocurrency is purely your decision, and that it is an educated decision. Don't be the person that invests in something, but can't articulate a basic understanding of the project.

7

Chapter 7: INVESTMENT STRATEGIES

Trading and Holding

There are two main types of investment strategies. Trading and holding. This is also true for other investments, but we will just talk about how it relates to cryptocurrency here.

Trading

Trading is the strategy of buying a cryptocurrency and holding it for less than a year with the purpose of selling it for a profit. Typically, traders will buy and sell a coin/token for profit within minutes, hours, or days. To be a good trader, you must watch a particular coin/token very closely in order to know when the price has dipped more than normal or whether it has increased more than normal. The idea is to buy when the coin/token price is low and sell it when the price is high to make money. Investors who trade are very knowledgeable about Technical Analysis (TA), which is an investment strategy used to predict what the market will do next based on reading charts. It operates under the assumption that the past will repeat itself.

The benefits of trading are that you can make money very fast. For example, if you invest $100 to buy a coin from an exchange for 1 cent a coin one day and sell it at 4 cents a coin the next day, you have turned that $100 to $400. That is easy money. Especially if the price of that coin increases drastically within hours or days, which happens very often in cryptocurrency. Compared to traditional markets, the cryptocurrency market is very volatile, and prices can go up or down 20% plus a day like its nothing. Traders try to take advantage of that to make money.

The downside of trading is that you can lose a lot of money fast if you guess wrong on predicting the price of a crypto. Many traders lose big time money when trading. It is all basically an educated guess as to when a price is going to increase or decrease in a period of time. So, if it is easy to make money, but it is also easy to lose it.

Another downside to trading is the amount of taxes you have to pay on your profits. The tax rate for trading (holding for a year or less) is much higher than if you hold the crypto for more than a year. So as a trader, you have to take that into account to determine if the trade is even worth the taxes you have to pay on it.

Holding

Holding or HODLing (Hold On For Dear Life) is the strategy of buying a cryptocurrency and holding it for longer than a year. At least a year and a day to be exact. Investors who hold tend to believe in the long-term prospects of a cryptocurrency. They believe that the crypto project they invested in will increase in price over the year or so that they hold it.

The benefits to holding is that the tax rate is lower than the trading tax rate. So, once you sell, you pay less taxes than a trader would on your profits. Also holding a cryptocurrency for over a year can give the crypto more time to grow; therefore, making the investor more profits than if they had sold earlier at a lower price.

The downside to holding is that the price of the crypto you invest in could also decrease significantly while you are holding it. This can cause an investor to lose money. But even then, if the investor still believes that the project will bounce back in a bull run or in bullish times, the investor can just hold it until they at least get their money back, or even make a good to great profit. You never know whether a crypto will recover in price enough for the investor holding it to get their money back.

Personally, I prefer holding because I do it with crypto projects that I truly believe in. The ones that I think will solve a problem in the world and grow significantly in price over time. Also, I love that I will pay less taxes on my profits than a trader would once I cash out. Holding just requires more patience.

Taxes

Now the IRS still doesn't quite know how to handle cryptocurrency as its own entity. They see cryptocurrency as property, not currency. So that means all cryptocurrency will be treated as any other property for tax purposes.

Now if you held your cryptocurrency for a year or less like a trader would, then you will have what the IRS calls a short-term capital gain or loss, which is the same as the income tax rate. Yep, every trade, whether it was big or small, or if you held the crypto for one minute or one year, you would have to pay short-term capital gains or loss tax. Look at the short-term capital gains tax bracket below and keep it in mind the next time you want to execute a trade, and determine if it will be worth it or not. Other cryptocurrency events like receiving payments, airdrops, mining coins, and staking are taxed as ordinary income.

Tax Rate	Single	Married Filing Jointly	Married Filing Seperately	Head of Household
10%	$0 - $9,875	$0 - $19,750	$0 - $9,875	$0 - $14,100
12%	$9,876 - $40,125	$19,751 - $80,250	$9,876 - $40,125	$14,101 - $53,700
22%	$40,126 - $85,525	$80,251 - $171,050	$40,126 - $85,525	$53,701 - $85,500
24%	$85,526 - $163,300	$171,051 - $326,600	$85,526 - $163,300	$85,501 - $163,300
32%	$163,301 - $207,350	$326,601 - $414,700	$163,301 - $207,350	$163,301 - $207,350
35%	$207,351 - $518,400	$414,701 - $622,050	$207,351 - $311,025	$207,351 - $518,400
37%	$518,401+	$622,051+	$311,026+	$518,401+

Short-Term Capital Gains Tax Bracket as of 2020.

Example: Let's say you are single and make $38,000 a year. You buy some Stellar (XLM) in June 2019 and sell it for a $100 profit in December 2019. Since you held Stellar (XLM) for less than a year, you will have to pay at the 12% tax rate.

If you held your cryptocurrency for a year and a day or longer, you would have to pay long-term capital gains or loss tax. A holder will likely pay less in taxes with long-term capital gains or loss tax. This is because the government wants investors to hold their investments for long periods of time. The incentive to hold is a lower tax bill on your profits.

Tax Rate	Single	Married Filing Jointly	Married Filing Seperately	Head of Household
0%	$0 - $40,000	$0 - $80,000	$0 - $40,000	$0 - $53,600
15%	$40,001 - $441,450	$80,001 - $496,600	$40,001 - $248,300	$53,601 - $469,050
20%	Over $441,451+	Over 496,601+	Over $248,301+	Over $469,051+

Long-Term Capital Gains tax as of 2020.

Example: Let's say you are single and make $38,000 a year. You buy some Stellar (XLM) in June 2018 and sell it for a $100 profit in July 2019. Since you held Stellar (XLM) for at least a year and a day, you won't have to pay any taxes at all because you are at the 0% tax rate.

So, in both scenarios, this single person making $38,000 a year invested in a cryptocurrency and sold it for a $100 profit. In one scenario they will have to pay 12% taxes on their profit, and in the other case, they won't have to pay any taxes on their profit. Which scenario would you prefer? 0% taxes of course. That is why you should hold on to your cryptocurrency investments for at least a year and a day if you can. It will make a huge difference in the amount of profits you keep.

Now if you have been holding a crypto for less than a year and the price is going up, and you want to sell, then sell. It's up to you. Just know that you will have to pay short-term capital gains taxes on it. Depending on how big your profits are, you may not care. Put yourself in the best position to make this decision quickly by keeping track of the dates you buy your crypto.

How to Cash Out

So you did your research, went to an exchange, purchased some cryptocurrency you believe in, the market caused it to increase in price, and now you want to cash out. I mean, you may believe like many other cryptocurrency enthusiasts that some cryptos like Bitcoin are the future of money; and you will always hold some and never sell it because Bitcoin itself will be the currency used to buy goods and services one day. I think that is a great idea. I plan to never sell some of my Bitcoin. But we're not there yet. And not every cryptocurrency will be here in the future or are meant to be a form of currency. So what many crypto investors do is turn their crypto into US dollars.

There are some crypto exchanges that allow you to trade your crypto for US dollars. When I cash out, I will be using Coinbase or Voyager. It depends on which one charges the least amount of fees to withdraw my US dollars into my checking account.

Let's run through a scenario. Let's say you bought some Ethereum (ETH) a while ago and now you want to cash out. But your ETH is on another exchange or in your wallet hopefully. All you need to do is send your ETH to a site like Coinbase or Voyager, follow the simple directions to sell, and your ETH will then be exchanged back to US dollars. Go to your accounts, withdraw your US dollars, and send to your bank account.

But what if you made great profits with a lesser known cryptocurrency like Mainframe (MFT). You can't send MFT to Coinbase or Voyager because MFT isn't a cryptocurrency that they provide in their accounts. So you have to exchange MFT into a bigger, more popular crypto that does have an account on Coinbase or Voyager like Bitcoin or Ethereum. So, you would send the MFT tokens from your wallet to an exchange and trade it for Bitcoin or Ethereum or another cryptocurrency with an account on Coinbase or Voyager. It may be a good idea to trade it into a stable coin like USD Coin (USDC) in order to protect your investment from constant price changes. It is up to you. But for the sake of this example, let's say you sold your MFT tokens for Bitcoin on an exchange. You then send that Bitcoin to a site like Coinbase or Voyager and sell it for US dollars.

Cashing out is a moment that all of us want to experience in the cryptocurrency game. Be smart, make the right moves at the right time, be patient, and you could put yourself in the position to cash out one day soon.

Cash Out Spreadsheet

One piece of advice I recently heard from the YouTube channel Ready Set Crypto is that you should never invest in a cryptocurrency without knowing at what price you would sell it at. At first I wasn't on board with that idea because I thought that involved too much planning up front. But as I thought more about it, it makes perfect sense. Why? Because when the bull market comes and the prices are going up super-fast, you will have a better idea of how much money you will make if you sell at certain prices when you have planned ahead. This planning will help keep you calm and help you make better decisions on when to sell your crypto in the middle of the frenzy. This planning will also help you decide if you should sell or continue to hold in order to meet your goals.

So I recommend creating a Cash Out Spreadsheet. In the sheet, record what price you bought in at (position), how much you invested at that price, and a future exit position. An exit position is the price at which you sell your crypto. Based on your research on that cryptocurrency, estimate some realistic future price estimates as your exit positions. From the chart below you see that for this crypto, $2, $3, $4, and $5 are the realistic exit positions that I have come up with. At each exit position, you can see how much I would make if I sold. If you have a chart like this for each cryptocurrency you have invested in, then you can have a realistic idea of how much you can make, and set yourself up to make more informed decisions when your favorite crypto goes up in price.

Position	$0.0478			
$ Invested	$256.35			
Exit Position	$2.00	$3.00	$4.00	$5.00
$ Made	$10,725.94	$16,088.91	$21,451.88	$26,814.85

Cash Out Spreadsheet Example

CHAPTER 7: INVESTMENT STRATEGIES

How I'm Investing in Bitcoin

I am buying a small amount of Bitcoin every month until I see a significant price drop occur. Let me explain. First off, this is what I am doing because I think it is smart to invest in Bitcoin by buying the same dollar amount regularly over time. It is called dollar cost averaging. I am not saying you should follow this buying strategy too, but I believe that if you do, you will thank yourself decades from now.

What I did was set up my Voyager account to automatically buy a certain dollar amount of Bitcoin every month. It is not a lot of money, but I believe the price of Bitcoin now is very low compared to what it will be in the coming years, decades. So dollar cost averaging Bitcoin over time is a great idea to me. It is still very early in the life of Bitcoin and buying a little over time on a regular basis will allow me to accumulate more Bitcoin now, than if I waited for the price to be 50k plus for example. I already have high confidence in Bitcoin based on its price history. I will not wait until mass adoption occurs in the near future and the Bitcoin price is 50k or 100k. Buying Bitcoin even at those high prices is still smart but buying now is even smarter.

Now when the next bear market occurs and I see that the Bitcoin price will be dropping significantly and continually over many months, I will pause on buying Bitcoin at that time. Not because I am losing confidence in Bitcoin, but because I know that because it is a bear market, the price will come down even lower and I will wait until I see the price get steady at a lower price before I start buying again. And I will save the money

I planned to invest in it each month during the bear market and use it to buy Bitcoin at what I think is about the lowest price it will go. That way I can buy more Bitcoin somewhere at the bottom of the market, which is the best time to buy any cryptocurrency.

8

Chapter 8: CRYPTOCURRENCY METRICS

Cryptocurrency Metrics

Cryptocurrency metrics is all the numerical data that makes up the financial side of the cryptocurrency. Market capitalization, circulating supply, price, and 24-hour volume are some of the main entities we will focus on now. These numbers will tell you everything you need to know about the health and potential of a cryptocurrency, outside of actual research on the project. These entities will be the first pieces of data you will see about a cryptocurrency once you look it up on the coin market cap site or any coin market cap app. If you buy a cryptocurrency, you will be checking these data points regularly to see how your investments are doing. See the definitions below to get an understanding of the phrases.

Market Capitalization - a measure of value for a cryptocurrency. Price x Circulating supply = Market Capitalization. For

Example if a crypto has a circulating supply of 1,000 coins, and its current price is 0.10 cents per coin, then its Market Capitalization is $100.

Circulating supply – the number of coins or tokens that are currently circulating in the market and available to the public.

24-hour Volume – the total amount in US dollars traded in the last 24 hours to buy or sell a cryptocurrency.

Price – the value of a single coin or token of cryptocurrency.

Market cap, supply, and price are all mathematically related. Price x Circulating Supply = Market Capitalization. You can look up any cryptocurrency and do this math and you will see it pans out.

How To Use These Data Points

Market capitalization is used to rank all cryptocurrencies in the market from 1 to 5,000 plus. It shows value. Market cap is especially good when predicting the potential growth of a cryptocurrency.

Let's say you like Dash (DASH) as a digital currency. And you want to get an idea of how much it can grow if it really takes off and does well. And by grow, I mean increase in price. What you can do is compare Dash to another more valuable digital currency like Litecoin (LTC). You would compare Dash to Litecoin because they are both the same type of cryptocurrency (digital currency). You wouldn't compare two cryptocurrencies that are not the same type. For example, you wouldn't use a platform crypto to guess the market cap of a digital currency crypto. Litecoin has a higher market cap than Dash. So as of right now the Dash price is $162.35 with a market cap of $1,440,983,706.11. The Litecoin price right now is $137.13 with a market cap of $8,545,923,924.52. So ideally you can think what price would Dash be if it went from a 1.4 billion market cap to a 8.5 billion market cap like Litecoin, which is a similar kind of cryptocurrency. Well using the Price x Circulating Supply = Market Capitalization formula, you would divide the <u>potential</u> market cap of Dash $8,545,923,924.52 by the current Dash circulating supply of 8,875,991.46 and get a price of $962.81. So by applying the market cap of Litecoin (a more valuable digital currency) to Dash, and seeing the Litecoin market cap as a value that Dash can reach one day if it performs well, you can estimate a future Dash price of $962.81. That is about 5.9 times more than its current price of $162.35. If you truly believe in Dash, you could see this and like its potential growth and the 5.9 multiplier and want to invest.

This method is a good way of guessing the future price of a cryptocurrency based on the growth of another similar cryptocurrency. But remember, it is only a guess and it is not guaranteed that the crypto you like will one day grow as valuable as its more valuable competitor.

Now that you understand what market capitalization, supply, price, and 24-hour volume are, let's look at how this affects how you make money.

Price

The price of crypto is very important. When you invest, you eventually want the price to increase so you can make money. But the price is affected greatly by the circulating supply. The higher the circulating supply, the more volume (money from trading) needs to happen for the price to increase or decrease. If a crypto has a circulating supply of 1 billion, then there will need to be a lot more buying or selling volume for the price to go up or down than compared to a crypto with a circulating supply of 1 million. So a crypto with less circulating supply has a price that is more volatile (price goes up and down quicker and more frequently) than a crypto with a much higher circulating supply.

For example, let's take Bitcoin (BTC) and Cardano (ADA). Bitcoin has a very low circulating supply of about 18 million, so the price of Bitcoin moves up or down much faster than most coins/tokens. Cardano has a circulating supply of about 25 billion. This is considered a very high circulating supply and the price is not as volatile as Bitcoin at all. 1 million dollars of 24-hour volume will move the Bitcoin price more drastically than it would the Cardano price. When the Bitcoin price changes, it changes in dollars. When the Cardano price changes, it changes in cents.

This is why circulating supply is a very important factor when deciding what crypto to invest in to make money. I would suggest you invest in any project you truly believe in no matter the circulating supply. But investing in a crypto with a circulating supply in the millions will increase your chances of either making more money or losing more money. It is a risk. But I see it as a risk worth taking if you truly believe in that cryptocurrency. Chances are you won't see the price go up or down as fast with a crypto with a circulating supply in the billions. A lot more volume will have to be pumped into that crypto for the price to move.

Think of it like this. Let's say you have two rocks. One rock is 1 pound and the other is 100 pounds. If you put in the same amount of effort to move the 1 lb rock as you did in moving the 100 lb rock, you would move the 1 lb rock much quicker and easier than you would the 100 lb rock. It would take way more effort for you to move the 100 lb rock just as fast as you did with the 1 lb rock. Keep this in mind when investing.

So, if you are looking to invest in a crypto that has the potential to have more volatility or price action, invest in something with a circulating supply that is less than a billion. I like the 90-600 million range personally outside of Bitcoin. If the volume increases dramatically more on the buy side for a crypto with a circulating supply in this range, the price will shoot up much quicker, making you more money. Anything in the billions will move slower.

But also know that there are some crypto projects out there with circulating supplies in the billions that are so popular and successful that they will get the volume needed to make their price move as quick as some cryptos with circulating supplies in the millions. It's all about the volume. I do own some that are in the billions though. That is because I believe in those cryptos so much that I think the price will increase effectively enough for me to make great profits.

Chapter 9: FIAT VS CRYPTOCURRENCY

Crypto During the Pandemic

As I write this, the world is going through the COVID-19 pandemic. Because unemployment is at highs not seen since the Great Depression, the government is sending COVID-19 relief checks to all eligible Americans. There are millions of people out there right now struggling to make it every day, and they need this relief check, even though it is only enough for the short term. The problem is that the people that have bank accounts will receive their money faster through direct deposit if the IRS has their bank information. But like I mentioned earlier in the preface, there are many people who don't have bank accounts, but they do have mobile devices.

If the treasury department was to use a stable coin like USDC, it would have sent the money out to every eligible American in one day, with way less processing time and for way less cost to the government. No money would have needed to be wasted on printing prepaid debit cards. Just everybody go to one app, and get your money through a stable coin cryptocurrency sent to your public address. Then the people have a choice to convert it into US dollars, keep the crypto on the app, or convert the stable coin into another cryptocurrency. Cryptocurrency payments would have created more options for all Americans.

We are stuck in an old slow system. It is the people with no bank accounts who probably need the money the most and need it now! Now they will have to wait weeks or longer for their prepaid debit cards to arrive in the snail mail. Which they will have to wipe down with antibacterial wipes because of COVID-19. Crazy! Cryptocurrency works! It is more than practical, it is needed! And a pandemic does nothing but point out why the current way money is handled and how it is centralized is not what is needed anymore. We need decentralization!

"Printing Money"

When economic disasters happen like the stock market crash in 2008 or the mass job losses during COVID-19, the US government and many governments around the world bail out industries and sometimes the people by sending them relief money. In order to do this, they "print money." By "printing money" I mean they increase the volume of money into circulation. It is part of a process called quantitative easing. As the government continues to "print money" over the years to help in harsh economic times, the country gets into deeper debt and the US dollar becomes more and more devalued because so much is put into circulation. Now the US dollar is still relatively strong compared to other fiat currencies in the world, but it is getting weaker because of all this debt and "money printing." Bitcoin will increase in value because of its scarcity and other major factors. Remember, there will never be more than 21 million Bitcoin in circulation.

Americans are working hard to get something that allows us to function as a society, the US dollar. But with the country getting into deeper debt and several bailouts causing the government to keep "printing money", the US dollar is not as valuable as it used to be. So what I will do is keep getting and saving US dollars, only because it is the form of currency widely used in this country, but invest more into Bitcoin, to be ahead of the curve of the future of money. The thing is, most people in this world don't know this, and will keep working hard for something that is deteriorating. But now you know. So don't just believe me, DYOR!

Cryptocurrency Is Just Easier

My wife and I own a college rental property in a HBCU town. It is our first rental property and we plan to have many more. One of the challenges we faced right away was how we were going to collect the rent from these college students with the least amount of friction. Keep in mind this property is in another state and our property manager is my brother- in-law who currently attends the school and lives at the property. The students pay the rent for the whole semester with the refund check they get from the school. We didn't want the refund check to stay in their hands too long. We didn't want them to give our property manager cash or a check. We also didn't want to give them our bank account number so they could deposit the money directly to our account at the bank. We read that some other landlords did that, but if people have your bank account number, they can commit all kinds of fraud. All we wanted was a simple, quick, fee-less or very low fee (in the cents) way for the tenants to send us the money electronically. In order to get them to pay the rent electronically online with no fees for them, we would have to pay a monthly subscription fee for landlord software. We didn't want to have to pay anything to get our money. Now I know you may be thinking, "What about CashApp, Venmo, Stripe, or PayPal?" Well, if we used Paypal or Stripe, we would have had to pay a percentage fee. And we didn't want our tenants sending large amounts of money through Cash App or Venmo because of potential fraud and send limits. So we came up with two options, they could send the money for free using Zelle (a service with many banks that allows you to send money for free from bank account to bank account), or they could send it to us through a free landlord software we were using to keep records and communicate with the tenants. But it charged the tenants 2.75% of the rent amount as a fee to send the money to us. The tenants didn't want to pay the 2.75% fee which charged them about $80 just to pay the rent! So they used the free Zelle service, which we knew they would. But we discovered that there is also a send limit with Zelle. The tenants couldn't send no more than $500 a day as new users of the service.

So annoying. So one tenant just sent $500 a day through Zelle until the rent was paid. The other tenant paid with a cashier's check from their bank, gave it to our property manager, and he went to the bank and sent it directly to our bank account. Although the cashier's check sent to our bank account was free for everybody, it is just an inefficient process involving a trip to the bank by the tenant and property manager, and it is not a quick way to get our money at all. Now the 3rd tenant, well that was the worst. The tenant was going to pay with a cashiers check, but they found out they had a hold on their debit card and didn't know why. For whatever reason the bank had to send them a new card which would arrive in 5 business days. So now the tenant was late on the rent. Once the tenant received the new debit card, they went online and sent the money via a check to our property manager in the mail. Once the property manager finally received the check in the mail, he couldn't go to the bank and send it to us because all the banks were closed because of COVID-19. So he just held it for about a month. We didn't want to wait any longer for the banks to re-open so we had the property manager deposit the check into his personal account via mobile deposit and then send the money to us using Zelle at $500 a day until we got all the money. But then after finally getting the last tenants rent money in our account, our property manager called us in a panic because his bank account was in the negative. It turns out the property managers bank didn't clear the check for reasons we still don't know even though it was a cashiers check. How does a bank not clear a cashiers check!? So after my wife spent hours on the phone with the bank, we found out we needed to send the money back to our property manager via Zelle at $500 a day, and then call the tenant and ask them to have their bank reissue the check. And that is where we are now. We are waiting for the tenants bank to reissue the check, and we still don't have our money. This is all crazy right? All this to get money owed to us. It can be so inconvenient to make simple payments at times with fiat. The current money system is old and inefficient.

Now in the future, my wife and I have decided to just pay a tenant software $9 a month to keep track of the properties business and most importantly allow the tenants to pay their rent from their bank accounts directly with no fees for any body. But we have to pay $9 a month for that convenience.

Let me show you how this could have went much smoother, quicker, much cheaper, and less stressful for everybody. Now earlier in this book I touched on the subject of public addresses and private keys. The public address is the location of your cryptocurrency in the blockchain and can be made public to anybody, and the private keys are what you need to access your crypto in order to send it anywhere and should never be made public. Well a bank account number is the combination of both. Now that may seem efficient, but you shouldn't give your bank account number to people to send you money unless they are extremely trustworthy. But with cryptocurrency, you can give your public address out to anybody and receive crypto in your wallet in minutes, with fees that are so small you won't even notice. That's how I wish we could collect our rent. The tenants could easily convert the rent amount from US dollars to a stable coin like USDC in an app, then send it to our public stable coin address in minutes with very low fees. And we wouldn't have to pay $9 a month. I know you can do that now with Cash App, Venmo, and Zelle, but depending on how much you send, you will run into send and/or receive limits with either the service or the bank. The blockchain has no minimum or maximum send limits, low fees, no bank hours, and the blockchain is way more reliable than a money sending app. All the sender and receiver have to do is trust the blockchain, and if needed for a more complicated transaction, trust the smart contract on the blockchain to accomplish the transaction. Person to person, no middle man. Quicker, cheaper, more convenient, more freedom.

And that is why cryptocurrency, the blockchain, and smart contracts are needed. We need to be able to exchange peer to peer without 3rd party interference and high fees. They make sending and receiving money, which is YOUR MONEY way too difficult.

10

Chapter 10: CRYPTO DEFINITIONS AND SLANG

Some of these definitions also apply to traditional markets. But for the purpose of this book, I have defined them in the context of cryptocurrency.

Cryptocurrency Defintions

24-hour volume – the total amount in US dollars traded in the last 24 hours to buy or sell a cryptocurrency.

Altcoin – any cryptocurrency other than Bitcoin.

ATH – stands for "ALL Time High". The highest price that a cryptocurrency has ever reached.

Blockchain - a trusted network of computers that all have the same history of transactions.

Blockchain Explorer or Block Explorer - a search tool for blockchains. On the block explorer you can check your wallet balance just by entering your wallet's public address, see the status of a transaction, and check pretty much any transaction details on that blockchain.

Circulating supply – the number of coins or tokens that are currently circulating in the market and available to the public.

Coin – refers to any cryptocurrency that has its own blockchain. Bitcoin is a coin because it has its own blockchain.

Correction – a decline in the price of a cryptocurrency after its most recent peak.

Cryptocurrency - a digital currency that uses encryption techniques to control the creation of monetary units called coins or tokens.

Decentralization – the process where the decision making is removed from a central authority and that responsibility is instead given to a large community. No bank and no government involvement.

Decentralized Exchange – an exchange that allows you to connect your wallet directly to the exchange, buy your cryptocurrency, and then store the cryptocurrency directly on your wallet. You are exchanging directly with other users (peer-to-peer).

Desktop Wallet – a wallet kept on your desktop or laptop computer. It can be downloaded from websites.

ERC20 Token- a crypto token created using the Ethereum platform. Ex. Power Ledger is an ERC20 token.

Exchange – a business that allows customers to buy and sell cryptocurrencies. These cryptocurrencies can be traded for fiat or other cryptocurrencies.

Fork – when a cryptocurrency has a software update or upgrade. The new software can either be compatible or incompatible with the previous software.

Gas – the price required to successfully process a transaction or a smart contract on the Ethereum blockchain. It is also a cryptocurrency used to process transactions on the Neo blockchain.

Hard fork – when a cryptocurrency has a software update or upgrade, and the new software is not compatible with the previous software; therefore, creating two incompatible coins or tokens.

Hardware Wallet – a wallet that is a secure USB type device that can be plugged into any computer. It is not connected to the internet. Also referred to as "cold" storage. The most secure way to store your cryptocurrency.

Market Capitalization - a measure of value for a cryptocurrency. Price x Circulating supply = Market Capitalization. For example, if a cryptocurrency has a circulating supply of 1,000 coins, and its current price is 0.10 cents per coin, then its Market Capitalization is $100.

Maximum supply – the most amount of coins or tokens that will ever exist for a cryptocurrency. Once a cryptocurrency reaches its maximum supply cap, there won't be any more supply created.

Mining – the process in which transactions of a cryptocurrency are verified and added to the blockchain using computers (nodes). These computers compete with other computers to solve the next block using cryptography. Once the block is solved, the transaction is permanently added to the blockchain and the miner who solved the problem is rewarded with that cryptocurrency.

Mobile Wallet – a wallet kept on your mobile phone. It comes in the form of an app that you can download.

Online Wallet – a wallet created on a cryptocurrency wallet website.

Paper Wallet – a wallet where the private keys and public address is written or typed on a piece of paper. It is one of the more secure wallets because it is never connected to the internet. It is also known as a form of "cold" storage.

Private Keys – A string of alphanumeric characters that gives you access to your cryptocurrency and allows you to send your cryptocurrency to others. If it is lost, you can't send your crypto. Ex: Bi568JieDer671QWV97KLhu0924HbN-

MLPPI871Q3r6YuiNaqqZxFGjl9478lkmm1

Public Address – a string of alphanumeric characters that is used in sending and receiving cryptocurrency. To receive cryptocurrency, you need to give the sender your address. To send cryptocurrency, you need to know the receiver's address. Ex: 1J43GSWSiepsGjPnmQ8g6Ueuutkfs1zOBd

Recovery Passphrase – a list of 12-24 random words that is given to you once you create a wallet. It will allow you to recover your cryptocurrency if you ever forget or are not able to access your private keys.

Satoshis – the smallest unit of a bitcoin. 1 satoshi equals 0.00000001 bitcoin.

Smart contract – is a computer protocol on the blockchain that can self-execute the terms of an agreement without the need of a middleman. The details of the agreement are written into lines of code.

Soft Fork – when a cryptocurrency has a software update or upgrade, and the new software is compatible with the previous software; therefore, maintaining one token or coin.

Stable Coin – a coin that stays at the price of around $1. Most are supposedly backed by real fiat or US dollars in the bank. Stable coins are used to store money before buying and after selling crypto. The benefit of transferring your funds to a stable coin is that your money is not susceptible to the volatility of the market.

Token – refers to any cryptocurrency that is built using an existing blockchain. For example, any cryptocurrency built using the Ethereum platform is a token.

Total Supply – the amount of coins or tokens that exist, but not all are circulating and available to the public. There are several reasons why a cryptocurrency project would lock up or reserve many coins or tokens and not make them available to be sold to the public. Total supply is usually greater than circulating supply.

Wallet – a software program that stores private and public keys and enables you to send and receive cryptocurrency by interacting with multiple blockchains.

White paper – an official document written by a new cryptocurrency project outlining the problem they want to solve, the methodology to solve the problem, a description of the product, and how it will interact with the users.

Cryptocurrency Slang

Airdrop – when a crypto project distributes coins/tokens to the wallets of certain users for free. Mostly for promotional reasons, awareness, rewards, etc.

Bag Holder – an investor who has or had plans to hold their cryptos for a long period of time. Also a hodler.

Bear – a person that is pessimistic on the current state of the cryptocurrency market.

Bear Market – when prices are dropping significantly after recent highs for a long period of time because of rampant pessimism and negative investor sentiment on the crypto market.

Bull – a person that is very positive on the condition of the cryptocurrency market.

Bull Market – when prices are increasing significantly after recent lows for a long period of time because of widespread optimism and positive investor sentiment on the crypto market.

Bull Run – a sustained significant increase in crypto market prices.

Bull Trap – when the crypto market prices go up significantly, leaving some investors to believe that a bull run is occurring, when it is actually just a temporary price spike. Leaving some who FOMO'd in at that high price to lose some money when the price goes back down.

Buying the Dip – the strategy of buying a crypto at a time when it is at its lowest prices; or buying right when the price dips after a price increase. A good strategy for hodlers and traders.

Cold Storage – a wallet where your private keys and public address are stored offline. Hardware and paper wallets are considered cold storage.

CHAPTER 10: CRYPTO DEFINITIONS AND SLANG

Crypto – short for cryptocurrency.

Cypherpunk – someone who is a cryptocurrency activist, who believes that crypto can bring social and political change.

Dollar Cost Averaging – the strategy of buying a fixed dollar amount of crypto over a regularly scheduled period of time, no matter what the price may be. Investing in a 401(k) is a good example of dollar cost averaging.

DYOR – stands for "Do Your Own Research". This acronym is usually used to caution investors to do their own research before buying a crypto. It is not good to buy a crypto just based on the opinion or review of someone else.

Fiat – government issued money. Like the US dollar, Yen, Euro, etc.

FOMO – stands for "Fear of Missing Out". It describes the fear investors get when a cryptocurrency they want to invest in is steadily going up in price; and they buy in because they fear that if they don't at that time, the price will get too high. They fear they will miss out on the massive gains. FOMO is not a good way to buy crypto because it usually means you bought in at a high price.

FUD – Fear, Uncertainty, and Doubt. FUD is the spread of negative opinions and coverage of the cryptocurrency market. It has been suspected that some FUD in the media has been done on purpose to manipulate the market.

Going Long – plans to hold your cryptos for a long period of time to make a profit.

Going Short – plans to sell a crypto within a short period of time, and then buy it back later at a lower price.

Hodl – in 2013, someone in a Bitcoin forum made a typo trying to spell the word "hold". It caught on. Now it is short for "Hold on For Dear Life". A term used to inspire or tell a cryptocurrency investor to hold their crypto for the long term.

Hodler – a person who has plans to hold their crypto for the long term.

Lambo – short for Lamborghini. It represents getting rich from cryptocurrency profits and buying something as expensive as a Lamborghini.

Maximalist – someone who has extreme views on a cryptocurrency. They can be bearish, bullish, outspoken, or passionate. For example, there are Bitcoin maximalists that only believe in Bitcoin and don't believe any altcoins will survive.

Moon – the optimistic idea of cryptocurrency prices rising to very high levels. "When moon?", "To the moon!"

Newbie – a person that is new to cryptocurrency.

OCD – Obsessive Cryptocurrency Disorder. When someone is obsessively checking the crypto market.

Pump and Dump – when the price of a cryptocurrency goes up quickly after the announcement of good news, and then goes down quickly due to large selling volume. The investors who purchased at a lower price sell and make a good profit, but FOMOers tend to buy in too late and lose money.

Rally – when a cryptocurrency or entire market has a time of continuous price increases.

Rekt – pronounced "wrecked." When an investor loses a lot of money in a bad trade or if the market takes a huge downturn.

Shill/Shilling – when someone talks very positively of a crypto for their own benefit, while misleading others.

Sh*tcoin – a crypto seen as a bad project, pointless, or a scam.

TA – Technical Analysis. An investment strategy used to predict what the market will do next. It operates under the assumption that the past will repeat itself.

Weak Hands – investors who are easily scared away by a volatile market and sell their cryptos at a loss instead of being patient and waiting for the prices to recover.

Whale – a crypto investor who is very wealthy and can drastically influence the cryptocurrency prices depending on if they buy or sell. They usually buy millions of dollars worth of crypto and can also sell millions of dollars worth of crypto.

Congratulations, you have now separated yourself from the

pack of billions, into a higher position of knowledge. You have read this book and know the basics of cryptocurrency. What are you going to do now? End your education here? No! Go on and Do Your Own Research! Learn more! Get even more familiar with the world of cryptocurrency and how it will affect your life, your family's life, and the world. If you choose, after doing some research, invest. Crypto Your Mind!

If you enjoyed this book, follow me on Instagram and Twitter @CryptoYourMind.

About the Author

Lawrence grew up in Stone Mountain, GA and graduated with a degree in Mechanical Engineering from Tuskegee University. Lawrence is married to an amazing wife Taneya and currently has one son, Dominic. He and his wife are very active in their local church. He is a Mechanical Engineer and real estate investor. Lawrence became interested in cryptocurrency when trying to figure out a creative way to quickly pay off his student loans. But when he dove deeper into the world of cryptocurrency, he found a much greater purpose. He discovered that he needs to inform as many people as he can about the basics of cryptocurrency so that they will not be left behind and be able to have the knowledge to catch the next wave of technology.

www.ingramcontent.com/pod-product-compliance
Lightning Source LLC
Chambersburg PA
CBHW050243220526
45465CB00002B/535